AMERICA
PAST AND PRESENT

Thunder Bay Press
An imprint of Printers Row Publishing Group
9717 Pacific Heights Blvd, San Diego, CA 92121
www.thunderbaybooks.com • mail@thunderbaybooks.com

Printers Row Publishing Group is a division of
Readerlink Distribution Services, LLC.

Thunder Bay Press is a registered trademark of
Readerlink Distribution Services, LLC.

Correspondence regarding the content of this book should be sent to Thunder
Bay Press, Editorial Department, at the above address. Author, illustration and
rights inquiries should be addressed to Bright Press at the address below.

Thunder Bay Press
Publisher: Peter Norton
Associate Publisher: Ana Parker
Editor: Dan Mansfield

This book was conceived, designed, and produced by
The Bright Press, an imprint of the Quarto Group,
1 Triptych Place, London SE1 9SH, United Kingdom.
www.quarto.com

The Bright Press
Publisher: James Evans
Editorial Director: Isheeta Mustafi
Art Director: James Lawrence
Managing Editor: Jacqui Sayers
Senior Editor: Dee Costello
Project Editor: Anna Southgate
Senior Designer: Emily Nazer
Design: Tony Seddon
Picture Research: Katie Greenwood
Text: Robin Pridy

Library of Congress Cataloging-in-Publication data available on request.

ISBN: 978-1-6672-0514-4

Printed in Malaysia

27 26 25 24 23 1 2 3 4 5

AMERICA

PAST AND PRESENT

THUNDER BAY
P·R·E·S·S

San Diego, California

CONTENTS

INTRODUCTION

PAST AND PRESENT America is a constantly changing landscape, and on a day-to-day basis this can be hard to notice. Yet a horse-drawn carriage driver in New York—a mere two human lifetimes ago—would not recognize today's Manhattan. So what can bear witness to these changes? Historical photographs can be a powerful tool—Boston's Old State House remains exactly as it was when built, but comparing a modern view to early photos shows the city's enormous growth around it.

America Past and Present aims to bear witness to these changes, from the Hoover Dam's incredible engineering to the grand vision of Disneyland and the majesty of Niagara Falls. And while it is just a selection of American places, they can also reveal our shifting understanding of the United States—from a wilderness to conquer to one to cherish and preserve, from conflicts over American Indian territory and the legacy of slavery to one of reconciliation. With these images, we hope to show you America, both past and present, looking to an even brighter future.

▶ Past and present photographs allow you to see at a glance changes that have occurred over the years. Here, at New York's Grand Central Terminal, for example, the building's facade is unchanged, while Pershing Square—a bus station in the past—is now pedestrianized.

The historic photographs in this book are genuine and the imperfections of their age only add to the richness of the stories they tell.

AMERICAN ICONS

OLD STATE HOUSE
BOSTON, MASSACHUSETTS

Located in the heart of downtown Boston, Old State House, built in 1713, is one of America's most historic public buildings. Originally known as the Town House, it served as the seat of British rule in America. The 7-foot-tall wooden statues of a lion and a unicorn flanking its east wall parapets were seen as powerful symbols of the British Empire. Yet the public mood shifted after a cold, snowy day on March 5, 1770, when British soldiers fired on protesters in the street out front, killing five and wounding many more. Known as the Bloody Massacre,

the event is widely recognized as being key in setting the course for the American Revolution. Six years later, on July 18, 1776, the American Declaration of Independence was read aloud from the Old State House balcony, to great celebration in the streets. A National Historic Landmark and part of America's famous Freedom Trail, today the Old State House functions as a history museum.

◀ Old State House, ca. 1900–10, with trolley lines on the cobbled streets out front; the cupola seen was once considered the highest point in the city.

▼ Today, the towering buildings of Boston's financial district engulf Old State House. A circle of pavers out front marks the spot where the Bloody Massacre took place.

STATUE OF LIBERTY
NEW YORK CITY, NEW YORK

Stepping out of broken chains, holding a tablet stating the date of the Declaration of Independence in one hand and a torch aloft in the other, sculptor Frédéric-Auguste Bartholdi's 151-foot-tall *Liberty Enlightening the World* has been gracing New York Harbor since June 19, 1885. A gift of friendship from France to celebrate America's recent emancipation of enslaved people, as well as the two countries' shared ideals of freedom, this "brazen giant of green fame" was meant to be shining gold. Less-expensive copper was chosen and, by 1906,

weathering had covered it in a distinctive green patina. Hailed as a masterpiece of art and engineering, its unique hollow metal framework, designed in part by Gustave Eiffel, can sway in strong winds and expand and contract with changing temperatures. Lady Liberty's body is covered in 310 thin, hand-hammered, riveted copper sheets, while her torch—a 1986 replacement of the original—is finished with more than 5,000 sheets of 24-carat gold leaf.

◄ An aerial view of Liberty Island, ca. 1936. The crowd is likely watching President Franklin D. Roosevelt rededicate the statue for its fiftieth anniversary.

▲ Under the care of the National Parks Service, the statue has undergone steady improvements, including better pedestal access and a new jetty. An American Museum of Immigration has replaced workers' housing.

◀ Statue of Liberty in 1905 and today. A metal plaque, added to its pedestal in 1903, holds Emma Lazarus's poem: "The New Colossus," welcoming "your huddled masses yearning to breathe free." Between 1892 and 1926, more than 18 million immigrants entered the United States, often arriving at Ellis Island. Many came by boat, with the Statue of Liberty the first thing they saw on arrival. Throughout the world, it is recognized as a beacon of freedom.

► St. Patrick's Cathedral, ca. 1894. Fifteen years after opening its doors, the church still towered above nearby buildings, briefly becoming New York's tallest when its 100-foot spires were added in 1888.

►► Though surrounded by skyscrapers today, "America's Parish Church" remains imposing. A 2014 restoration made 30,000 repairs, among them returning the marble facade to gleaming white and restoring all 3,200 panels of stained glass.

ST. PATRICK'S CATHEDRAL
NEW YORK CITY, NEW YORK

In 1858, John Hughes, Archbishop of New York, laid the first cornerstone for St. Patrick's Cathedral, in what was still considered wilderness, convinced it would soon become the heart of the city; the press called it "Hughes' Folly." Today, what is now an International Historic Landmark occupies an entire city block on Fifth Avenue in midtown Manhattan. At around 40,000 square feet, it remains North America's largest Gothic Revival Catholic cathedral, able to hold 2,400 people. The cathedral's enormous bronze doors—each weighing more than 9,000 pounds but designed to be opened with one hand—first opened in 1879, twenty-one years after construction began.

EMPIRE STATE BUILDING
NEW YORK CITY, NEW YORK

The 102-story Empire State Building, built between 1930 and 1931, was the world's tallest building for more than forty years, until the nearby World Trade Center was completed in 1973. Built during the Great Depression, the "empty state building," as it became known, did not become profitable until 1950. An extensive renovation has reinstated interior marble walls and an Art Deco ceiling, and an energy-saving refit has reduced the building's emissions by 40 percent. A new LED system can emit 16 million possible colors into the night sky.

◀ Looking south from the observation deck at the Rockefeller Center, 1950s. The Empire State Building dominates the midtown Manhattan skyline, with the view across New York Harbor showing little development.

▲ This same view of the building, taken in 2018. The city skyline shows the Empire State Building to be just one of several large skyscrapers in Manhattan today, with more under construction.

► The seventeen-story Waldorf-Astoria Hotel, completed in 1897 at Fifth Avenue and 33rd Street, was demolished in 1929 to make way for the Empire State Building. Popular with celebrities, the hotel boasted a telephone in every room, while its restaurant famously created Waldorf salad, eggs Benedict, and Thousand Island dressing.

►► The Empire State Building in construction stages (1930–31) and in 2018. Built to 1,250 feet in just 410 days by more than 3,400 workers, the Art Deco skyscraper features an iconic spire originally designed to moor airships. A 222-foot antenna was added in 1950, and the current, shorter one takes the building's full height to 1,454 feet.

BROOKLYN BRIDGE
NEW YORK CITY, NEW YORK

When completed in 1883, the Brooklyn Bridge became the first fixed crossing over the East River, the first to use steel cables, and the world's longest suspension bridge, spanning 1,595 feet. Although designed by engineer John Augustus Roebling, an on-site accident contributed to his death before the first stone was laid in 1869. Completion of his work fell to Roebling's son, Washington. When Washington himself was left partially paralyzed (after succumbing to decompression sickness while working on the bridge's underwater foundations), he enlisted

the help of his wife, Emily Warren Roebling. Fourteen years later, Emily crossed into Manhattan by carriage, carrying a rooster on her lap as a symbol of victory. Sadly, six days after opening, rumors about safety caused a stampede that left twelve dead. In response, showman P. T. Barnum successfully crossed the bridge with twenty-one of his circus elephants. Later tests proved the structure was, in fact, six times stronger than it needed to be.

◄ A mid-twentieth-century view of the Brooklyn Bridge. Its first major upgrade, in 1948, saw the bridge's trusses and steel cables modernized and two lanes of wooden-block roadway widened to six concrete lanes.

▲ View of the Brooklyn Bridge, looking across the East River toward the city, with Brooklyn Bridge Park in the foreground, 2015. The six-lane bridge carries 150,000 vehicles, pedestrians, and cyclists between Manhattan and Brooklyn daily.

◄ Looking south toward
Manhattan, with
commuters on the raised
timber promenade,
ca. 1910 and 2019. Despite
multiple upgrades, the
bridge remains largely
unchanged. Four
galvanized steel cables
(each the diameter of
a large pizza) continue
to support the deck,
and more than 1,500
suspender cables form
the beautiful latticework
that has inspired many
poets and artists.

INDEPENDENCE HALL
PHILADELPHIA, PENNSYLVANIA

Over the course of two hot July days in 1776, fifty-six delegates from thirteen colonies met in the Assembly Room of Pennsylvania State House—now known as Independence Hall—to debate, then vote on, their independence from Great Britain. In defiance of King George III, they chose liberty, writing the American Declaration of Independence in risk of "their lives, their fortune, and their sacred honor." Eleven years later, the United States Constitution was signed in this same room. A UNESCO World Heritage Site today, the building

became a more somber backdrop in 1865, when more than 300,000 mourners came to pay their respects at President Abraham Lincoln's open coffin. Only four years earlier, the president-elect had spoken in the hall, professing his hope that "in due time, the weights should be lifted from the shoulders of all men, and that all should have an equal chance."

◄ Independence Hall, ca. 1905, seen from the north side across Chestnut Street and flanked by Congress Hall (right) and Old City Hall (left). Built of brick in the Georgian style, the building was threatened with demolition in 1816, but saved.

▼ Independence Hall—familiar from the back of the U.S. $100 bill—remains relatively unchanged, though it is now part of Philadelphia's 55-acre Independence National Historical Park, a string of sites associated with the American Revolution.

◄ The Liberty Bell, suspended in the foyer at Independence Hall, ca. 1905. Today, the bell hangs in the Liberty Bell Center, built in 2003, directly across the road. Its inscription from the Bible, "Proclaim liberty throughout all the land unto all the inhabitants thereof," inspires millions.

WASHINGTON MONUMENT
WASHINGTON, DISTRICT OF COLUMBIA

Standing more than 555 feet tall, once completed in 1884, the Washington Monument obelisk was the world's tallest artificially made structure—an honor it held until the construction of the Eiffel Tower in Paris five years later. The granite structure took thirty-six years to finish and is faced with two kinds of Maryland marble. The capstone alone weighs 3,300 pounds and the entire structure an estimated 91,000 tons. Visitors can walk the 897 steps to the observation deck or ride in the elevator, a journey that takes sixty seconds.

◄ In 1934, scaffolding covered the monument for its fiftieth anniversary restoration, enabling engineers to examine the gold-plated, platinum-tipped lightning rods and aluminum cap at its apex.

▲ Looking south toward the Washington Monument today. Its location is the exact surveyed center of the original District of Columbia. The U.S. Capitol sits directly to the west, and the White House directly to the north.

Ice skating, ca. 1920s
and now, with the
Washington Monument
in the distance. Although
prohibited, skaters,
sledders, and even ice
hockey players take their
chances on the ice when
the reflecting pools on the
National Mall freeze over.

CAPITOL BUILDING
WASHINGTON, DISTRICT OF COLUMBIA

Set within 131 acres of grounds in Washington, D.C., the Capitol Building has been home to the U.S. Senate and the House of Representatives for more than 200 years. Construction first began in 1793, largely using the labor of enslaved African Americans, and though Congress first sat there in 1800, building work lasted until 1826. During this time, it was partially burned down by the British during the War of 1812 (a sudden rainstorm saved it), only to be rebuilt. From the 1850s through 1869, it was greatly extended and the

copper-clad dome replaced. Construction halted during the Civil War, when it served as a bakery, military barracks, and hospital for Union soldiers—twenty ovens were supposedly installed in the basement for baking bread. Abraham Lincoln was the first of twelve presidents to lie in state in the Rotunda, the circular room that sits beneath the Capitol dome. Others to have laid there in state, or in honor, include Ruth Bader Ginsburg, Rosa Parks, and John F. Kennedy.

◄ Troops march in front of the Capitol Building, April 1, 1920. The dome was modeled by architect Thomas Walter on Michelangelo's Roman masterpiece, the dome of St. Peter's Basilica. A 19.5-foot-tall bronze statue, *Freedom*, stands atop.

▼ In 2016, the Capitol's 540 rooms, including statues, paintings, and ceilings, were extensively restored, as was the dome. Today, the building also houses the Capitol Visitor Center, a large underground extension built in 2008.

▶ The Willis Tower, known as the Sears Tower until 2009, not long after its completion in 1974. The world's tallest building until 1996, its construction used vertical steel tubes designed to withstand high winds and limit sway.

▶▶ The Willis Tower today, at dusk. The 280-foot twin antennae, added in 1984, now light up at night. Extensive renovations have introduced shopping space, a rooftop terrace, and a glass observation box. The new elevators can rise 1,200 feet in 60 seconds. Since 2009, the tower has hosted the world's largest indoor stair climb.

WILLIS TOWER
CHICAGO, ILLINOIS

The views from Chicago's 110-story Willis Tower—one of the world's tallest skyscrapers—can take in four states, extending 50 miles. Sheathed in black aluminum, and with more than 16,000 bronze-tinted windows, 104 elevators, and square space equivalent to 101 football fields, this testament to engineering opened in 1973 and took more than 2,000 workers to build. An observation deck on the 103rd floor, at 1,353 feet, had four fully enclosed, retractable glass boxes added in 2009—each extends 4.3 feet from the building and has been designed to hold five tons.

GATEWAY ARCH
ST. LOUIS, MISSOURI

Forming part of a national park that sits on the west bank of the Mississippi River, the Gateway Arch commemorates the Louisiana Purchase of 1803, which doubled the size of the United States. A nationwide design competition in 1948 first determined what shape the monument would take and, in 1963, construction began on the 630-foot stainless-steel arch. Designed by Eero Saarinen, the arch represents a catenary curve—the shape made by a free-hanging chain suspended from two fixed points. The distance between the two legs at the base of the arch is equal to its height.

◀ **October 28, 1965. Spectators watch cranes maneuver the arch's final section into place. In the background, the Old Courthouse was the site of a case involving Dred Scott, who sued the state for his freedom as an enslaved person. The ruling against him, which went to the Supreme Court, is thought to have hastened the Civil War.**

▶ Still the tallest monument in the United States, the arch today is feted as a showcase of mid-century modern design, with visitors able to take a tram to a viewing platform at the top.

MOUNT RUSHMORE
BLACK HILLS, SOUTH DAKOTA

Carved in granite between 1927 and 1941 by Gutzon Borglum, Mount Rushmore consists of the 60-foot faces of former U.S. presidents George Washington, Thomas Jefferson, Theodore Roosevelt, and Abraham Lincoln. At the time of its conception, women's rights advocate Rose Arnold Powell tried to have a likeness of suffragist and human rights activist Susan B. Anthony on the mountain, but to no avail. More than 400 miners and laborers worked on the project, using dynamite, jackhammers, and detonators to blast away the rock before

sculpting could begin with finer carving tools. Workers, some of whom were young boys, climbed the 700 steps up the mountain, to be lowered in front of the 500-foot rock face by a ⅜-inch cable. In 1980, the U.S. government was sued for illegal seizure of the land on which Rushmore sits. Eight American Indian tribes won $100 million in compensation. The Lakota tribe calls the mountain Tunkasila Sakpe Paha, or Six Grandfathers Mountain, and they consider it a place of devotion, as well as a place to meet and to gather food.

◄ Mount Rushmore's faces under construction, 1930s. George Washington's figure was completed in 1930, Jefferson's in 1936, and Lincoln's in 1937, though his beard is not finished in this image. Roosevelt was not completed until 1939.

▲ Today, more than 2 million people visit Mount Rushmore each year. Borglum's long-abandoned dream of a Hall of Records inside the monument was achieved in 1998, with historic documents and objects stored for future visitors.

ALAMO MISSION
SAN ANTONIO, TEXAS

Originally known as the chapel of the Mission San Antonio de Valero, the Alamo Mission was founded by Franciscan monks between 1716 and 1718. It had been a partial ruin set in a grove of cottonwood trees (*alamo* is Spanish for cottonwood) before its reoccupation in the 1800s, first by Spanish troops and then by a group of volunteer soldiers fighting for independence against the Mexican government. This last occupation turned into the 1836 Battle of the Alamo, with around 190 men, women, and children surrounded by up to 6,000 Mexican

government troops. Only about fifteen people, mostly women and children, were spared by the Mexican troops, who also suffered large casualties. "Remember the Alamo!" became a popular battle cry among U.S. soldiers in the Mexican–American War of 1846–48, and has entered popular culture as a phrase to symbolize resistance.

◀ The Alamo Mission, 1880. Part of the barracks (left) became a large museum and general store, and a commercial center for San Antonio as it grew. In 1883, the state of Texas purchased the Alamo Mission for its preservation.

▼ Now a UNESCO World Heritage Site, the Alamo Mission is managed by the Daughters of the Republic of Texas, a women's organization formed of Texan-pioneer descendants.

CAPITOL RECORDS
LOS ANGELES, CALIFORNIA

This thirteen-story building, just north of the Hollywood and Vine intersection in Los Angeles, was once called "a monstrous stack of records" by the press due to its unique circular design. It is now a Hollywood landmark, a backdrop for the Walk of Fame, and home to some of America's most famous recordings by the likes of Nat "King" Cole and the Beach Boys, among others. Its studio features echo chambers 30 feet underground, with seven layers of walls that can keep reverb for up to five seconds.

◄◄ The corner of Hollywood Boulevard and Vine Street at night, ca. 1958. At its opening in 1956, the red light atop the Capitol Records spire was turned on by Samuel Morse's granddaughter Leila—blinking out the word "Hollywood" in Morse code, which it still does to this day.

◄ The Capitol Records Building today. Its south wall was restored in 2011, using hand-painted ceramic tiles. It features a mural first created in 1990, showing jazz greats from Billie Holiday and Miles Davis to Chet Baker and Ella Fitzgerald.

GRAUMAN'S CHINESE THEATRE
LOS ANGELES, CALIFORNIA

Host to countless movie premieres, including *Star Wars* in 1977, this is one of the world's most famous movie theaters. Built in 1927 and designed to resemble a red Chinese pagoda, the theater had to request permission from the U.S. government to import temple bells, pagodas, and other artifacts from China, including the giant stone heaven dogs that remain today. Its lavish design includes lotus-shaped fountains and carved stone dragons beneath copper turrets and a bronze roof.

◀ Grauman's Chinese Theatre in 1927, the year it first opened. The first movie shown, *King of Kings*, by Cecil B. DeMille, played for five months, drawing 500,000 theatergoers.

▲ Known as the TCL Chinese Theatre since 2013, the main auditorium is now a giant IMAX theater. About 2 million people visit each year, hoping to find their favorite star's hand- and footprints in the cement of the forecourt.

GOLDEN GATE BRIDGE
SAN FRANCISCO, CALIFORNIA

The bright orange, 1.7-mile-long Golden Gate Bridge is synonymous with San Francisco. Built in 1937, it was the world's longest suspension bridge for twenty-seven years, connecting the city with Marin County to the north. To announce its first day of opening, U.S. president Franklin D. Roosevelt pressed a telegraph key from the White House and "every siren in San Francisco and Marin was sounded, every church bell rang, ships sounded their whistles, and every fog horn blew." An estimated 15,000 visitors per hour crossed the

bridge that day, with around 50,000 hot dogs sold to hungry pedestrians. Designed to withstand strong winds, the bridge, which weighs about 887,000 tons, can move 15 feet vertically and 27 feet side to side. Remarkably, only eleven workers died during construction, thanks in part to a safety net placed below the deck. The nineteen men whose lives it saved called themselves the "Halfway to Hell Club."

◄ **Construction of the Golden Gate Bridge, 1934, with the first of its 746-foot towers built. A bridge of this span was initially thought impossible here due to fog, winds, strong tides, and deep water in the strait.**

▼ **The Golden Gate Bridge today. Its distinctive orange color was partly chosen for its visibility in fog, but also for its pleasing contrast to the blue sky and ocean, and its blending in with the Marin County hills.**

▲ The Golden Gate Bridge, ca. 1935, with Marin County in the distance. The bridge is shown here with towers and cables in place. Each main cable is more than 3 feet in diameter, and consists of 61 bundles of around 450 thin steel wires packed tight. That's more than 27,000 wires within one cable.

▲ The bridge today. Restorations have included replacing all 250 pairs of vertical ropes and ugrading the deck with a lighter steel-plate design. Around 112,000 vehicles cross daily; in 1985, the billionth driver made the crossing, receiving a hard hat and a case of champagne.

ALCATRAZ
SAN FRANCISCO, CALIFORNIA

For twenty-nine years between 1934 and 1963, 22-acre Alcatraz Island was the site of America's most notorious maximum-security prison. Sitting isolated in the Golden Gate strait 1.5 miles from San Francisco, "the Rock" was surrounded by deep, cold, and famously treacherous currents that proved the perfect deterrent for anyone trying to escape. Few tried, and none are officially known to have gotten away alive. Prior to this, it was a haven for birds, known as the "Isla de los Alcatraces," or the "Island of the Pelicans," and featured the

first lighthouse on California's coast. In its role as a military prison in the late 1800s, it held American Indian prisoners from many different tribes, including those who refused to put their children into government-run education programs. By 1912, the prison complex was the largest reinforced-concrete building in the world. In 1969, American Indian activists occupied the now-abandoned Alcatraz for nineteen months, beginning the American Indian Red Power movement.

◀ Alcatraz Island in 1938, with San Francisco in the distance. Four years previously, it had become a maximum-security federal penitentiary. Each cell was about 10 by 4.5 feet and housed criminals such as Al Capone and "Machine Gun" Kelly.

▲ Today, Alcatraz Island is a tourist attraction, administered by the National Parks Service. While it was a prison, there were never more than 250 prisoners at any one time. It now attracts more than 1.5 million visitors a year.

AMERICA AT LEISURE

CONEY ISLAND
NEW YORK CITY, NEW YORK

Famed for its 3.5-mile boardwalk, amusement rides, and the ever-present smell of grilled hot dogs, Coney Island was first inhabited by the Lenape tribe, who called it Narrioch, or "land without shadows," thanks to its sunny south-facing beaches. Used by English colonists as a grazing site for animals, its set of islands was only accessible at low tide until silting and infill made it part of the mainland. By the late 1800s, its popularity as a sea-bathing resort grew among middle-class travelers, including Herman Melville, who is believed to have written

Moby-Dick here in 1849. Amusement rides such as the Human Roulette Wheel, which placed riders in the middle of a spinning disk, and the arrival of the subway in 1920, cemented its place as the "people's playground." Until World War II, it was the nation's largest amusement area. Now a mix of housing, amusement areas, and beachfront, it has seen renewed popularity since a lull in the postwar period.

◄ Despite its decline, Coney Island still drew thousands of beachgoers in 1966. Seen on the far left is one of its first rides, the steel-framed 262-foot-high Parachute Jump that opened in 1939; it remained in operation until 1968.

▼ Coney Island today, with new and old amusement rides and entertainment features, including the defunct Parachute Jump, now on the National Register of Historic Places.

▶ Nathan's hot dog stand, 1954, its signage taking over a corner of Coney Island's boardwalk. Polish immigrant Nathan Handwerker opened his stand in 1916. He charged a nickel per hot dog, having borrowed $300 from friends and pilfering his wife's grandmother's spice recipe as a secret ingredient.

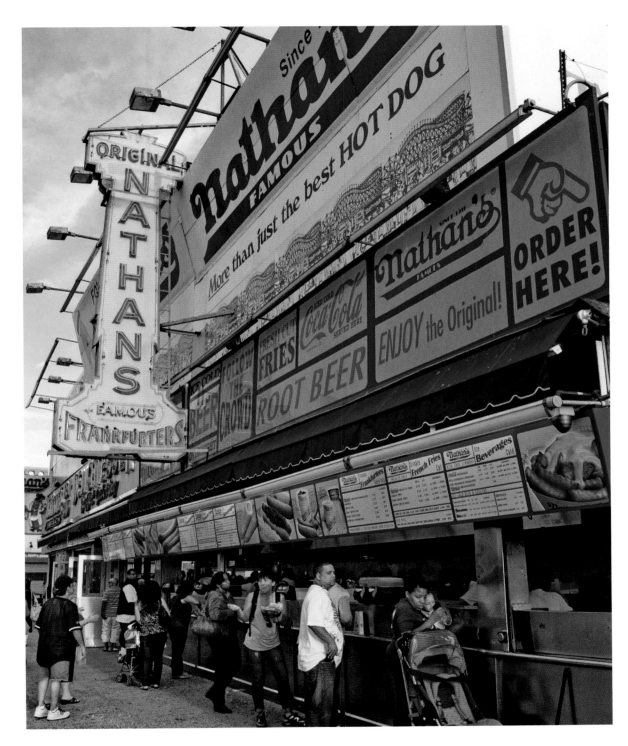

◄ Nathan's, still popular today. Now over 100 years old, it is considered to be one of the world's largest hot dog stands. Each year, it hosts a famous Hot Dog Eating Contest, watched by around 1 million on TV, where competitors have ten minutes to eat the most hot dogs, including the buns.

YANKEE STADIUM
NEW YORK CITY, NEW YORK

Home of the New York Yankees baseball team, the first Yankee Stadium, built in 1923, was also known as "the house that Ruth built," after the team's legendary slugger Babe Ruth. The original three-tiered stadium—with its distinctive green patina on the copper frieze that hung from part of the roof— was also host to several boxing, football, and soccer games as well as musical concerts and religious events. Thanks to Ruth and the likes of Lou Gehrig, Joe DiMaggio, Reggie Jackson, and Mickey Mantle, the Yankees managed to win twenty-six

World Series in the old stadium over the course of eighty-five years. Its seating was officially 58,000, but at times it hit crowds of 80,000. Renovations in the 1970s included baseball's first instant-replay display, or "telescreen." In 2009, the Yankees moved to a new $2.3 billion stadium built across the street, winning the World Series in their first year there.

◀ View of the original Yankee Stadium, newly built in 1923. The irregular shape of the field was designed to favor left-handed hitters like Babe Ruth, with the right field bleachers even named "Ruthville" by fans.

▲ The 2009 state-of-the-art, 51,000-seat Yankee Stadium, with extra parking and the addition of a subway station, includes sixty luxury boxes, a restaurant and bar complex, and a museum. The old stadium site is now a public park.

CHURCHILL DOWNS
LOUISVILLE, KENTUCKY

Churchill Downs racetrack is home to the Kentucky Derby horse race, a 1¼-mile race for three-year-old thoroughbreds that takes place in May each year. The site itself was the idea of Meriwether Lewis Clark Jr.—grandson of famous explorer William Clark—who wanted to build the 1-mile-circumference track on 80 acres of land owned by his uncles, John and Henry Churchill. Its main event continues to be the Kentucky Derby, known as "the greatest two minutes in sports" (though only two horses have ever finished in under two minutes). This

alone can draw as many as 170,000 spectators in one day. The derby's first race, in 1875, was won by a horse named Aristides, ridden by jockey Oliver Lewis. Aristides's life-size bronze statue stands in the clubhouse gardens. Thought to be America's longest-continuing sporting event, the derby is also called "The Run for the Roses," thanks to the garland of 400 red roses received by the winner.

◄ Churchill Downs during the 1943 Kentucky Derby. Originally a race of 1½ miles, this was reduced to 1¼ miles in 1896. Its location 3 miles south of Louisville and alongside the railroad tracks proved ideal for transporting horses.

▼ Today, Churchill Downs, with its trademark twin spires, is a National Historic Landmark. A $190-million, three-year renovation project aims to greatly expand its guest space.

THE LINEUP FOR THE START
500 MILE RACE
INDIANAPOLIS MOTOR SPEEDWAY
MAY 30, 1911.

"CIRKUT" PHOTO
BY C.F. BRETZMAN
INDIANAPOLIS.

INDIANAPOLIS MOTOR SPEEDWAY
SPEEDWAY, INDIANA

Built in 1909, the Speedway's 2.5-mile banked oval track was initially made from crushed stone, gravel, and a tar and oil solution. After two fatal accidents, the track was replaced using more than 3 million bricks, giving it the name "The Brickyard." Its original grandstands fit 12,000—today, the 253-acre venue can hold 350,000, with about 235,000 permanent seats. A National Historic Landmark, the track was completely asphalted by 1938, bar the "Yard of Bricks," a 36-inch strip at the starting line.

◀ The starting line at the first Indianapolis 500 race, in 1911—winner Ray Harroun, in the Marmon "Wasp," took 6 hours, 42 minutes, and 8 seconds to finish the 200 laps, a distance of 500 miles.

▲ The Indianapolis 500, with 2022 winner Marcus Ericsson in the lead at the starting line, racing past the 92-foot scoring pylon. The 153-foot Pagoda observation tower was added in 2000. Seen at the right are the "Gasoline Alley" garages.

WRIGLEY FIELD
CHICAGO, ILLINOIS

Opened on the North Side of Chicago in 1914, Wrigley Field is the oldest standing National League ballpark. It has been home to the Chicago Cubs baseball team since 1916. Famed for its ivy-clad outfield walls and vintage hand-operated scoreboard, this National Historic Landmark started the tradition of allowing fans to keep balls fouled into the stands. It also broadcast the nation's first live game on radio in 1925. Known as the "Friendly Confines," Wrigley Field is in a mainly residential area, and has only allowed lighting for night games

since 1988. Its original seating capacity was 14,000, though this is now over 41,000; still, many of the owners of the buildings that overlook the stadium rent out their rooftops to fans during Cubs games. The Cubs had the longest championship drought in major league history, which lasted from 1908 until their exuberant 2016 victory over Cleveland.

◄ **Wrigley Field on October 10, 1945. Fans wait in line for tickets to the World Series final between the Detroit Tigers and the Chicago Cubs, which the Cubs lost. Many players still had not been discharged from active military service.**

▼ **Wrigley Field, 2006. The ballpark's Art Deco marquee has remained above the entrance for around ninety years. At first dark blue, it was painted red in the mid-1960s.**

DISNEYLAND
ANAHEIM, CALIFORNIA

Built on 160 acres of an Anaheim orange grove in 1955, Disneyland was the only theme park overseen by Walt Disney himself, with eighteen attractions in five sections: Main Street, U.S.A., Fantasyland, Frontierland, Adventureland, and Tomorrowland. The opening gala saw about 30,000 people enter, causing excessive crowding on a hot day, and high heels sinking into the newly poured sidewalks. The next day's public opening—entrance fee $1—saw crowds lining up from 2:00 a.m. Soon known as "the happiest place on Earth," the park today

has up to 18 million visitors a year and employs nearly 30,000 "cast members," around 600 of them working overnight to keep it pristine. The tapping heard at New Orleans Square station is a Morse code message of Walt Disney's live opening words on TV: "To all who come to Disneyland, welcome. Here age relives fond memories of the past, and here youth may savor the challenge and promise of the future."

◀ **Disneyland, ca. 1955.** Main Street, U.S.A., running down the park's center, was modeled on Disney's hometown of Marceline, Missouri.

▲ **Disneyland, 2021.** California Adventure Park replaced the original parking lot, but Main Street, U.S.A. remains almost unchanged. In Disney's personal apartment above the firehouse, an antique lamp in the window remains lit.

◀ Sleeping Beauty Castle
under construction, 1955,
and in 2009. Relatively
unchanged, this iconic
symbol of Disneyland
leads visitors from Main
Street, U.S.A. into
Fantasyland. Modeled
after Germany's
nineteenth-century
Neuschwanstein Castle,
its working drawbridge
has only been raised and
lowered twice.

LOS ANGELES COLISEUM
LOS ANGELES, CALIFORNIA

The 18-acre Los Angeles Memorial Coliseum, opened in 1923, has hosted two Summer Olympics and a vast range of sporting and cultural events since it was first commissioned as a World War I veterans memorial. The "Grand Old Lady," just 4 miles from downtown Los Angeles, has remained relatively unchanged over the years and is a stalwart of sporting events, having hosted three NFL Championships, two Super Bowls, and the 1959 World Series, as well as hundreds of soccer games. Because of its capacity—at times it has exceeded 100,000—it

has also seen extraordinary visits from the likes of Pope John Paul II, who performed the first Papal Mass here, as well as from Martin Luther King Jr. and Nelson Mandela. The Rolling Stones, Prince, and U2 have played here, and there has even been a NASCAR racing track and a ski jump within its oval. Upgrades have included two enormous videoboards and a military-grade sound system.

◀ The Coliseum during a football game, ca. 1931. After Los Angeles was awarded the 1932 Summer Olympics, the Coliseum increased its seating capacity to 105,500, though it is now under 80,000.

▼ An NFL game, 2019. The Olympic cauldron torch, seen here above the colonnade at the east end of the stadium, was added for the 1932 Olympic Games.

AMERICAN CITYSCAPES

BOSTON HARBOR
BOSTON, MASSACHUSETTS

A modern urban harbor today, this area's natural inlets and resources were used by American Indians for thousands of years for fishing, hunting, and planting crops. This changed when the harbor's strategic location as a port was discovered by European colonists. By the 1700s, members of the Massachusetts tribe had been forcibly removed and the harbor was active in the British Empire's Atlantic trade in enslaved people and traded goods. In 1773, colonists dumped British tea into the harbor in protest of excessive taxation. Known as the

Boston Tea Party, the event helped lead to the American Revolutionary War and by the 1800s, the harbor was instead serving as refuge to enslaved stowaways seeking freedom in the northern states. Rapid industrialization and untreated sewage in the 1900s saw its waters become severely polluted. However, a court-ordered cleanup of "the harbor of shame" in 1984 has resulted in great improvements.

◄ Boston Harbor, 1930s, with the Custom House Tower standing tall in the distance. At this time, the water was too polluted to fish or swim in.

▲ Boston Harbor, today. Other skyscrapers have joined the Custom House Tower. The harbor itself now has fishable and swimmable waters, with a marina and harborfront walk along the shoreline.

COLUMBUS CIRCLE
NEW YORK CITY, NEW YORK

Located at the southwest corner of Central Park, at the intersection of Eighth Avenue, Broadway, 59th Street, and Central Park West, Columbus Circle is the point from which all New York City's official highway distances are measured. Originally farmland that slowly became residential areas and then the theater district, the circle was first installed in 1892, with a monument to Christopher Columbus in its center. It was completely excavated in 1901 to construct the city's first subway line, its surface overlaid with wooden boards while

workers dug far below. In the late 1980s, after several failed attempts to improve the intersection, by then a jumbled flow of traffic with motorcycle parking in its center, the circle was redesigned. The project was completed in 2005 and now all traffic flows in a counterclockwise direction. The inner circle features an award-winning landscape with a water fountain, benches, new plantings, and a live-streaming webcam.

◄ **Aerial view of Columbus Circle, 1924.** The USS *Maine* National Monument can be seen at the southwest entrance to Central Park. This area grew slowly, with many tenement buildings remaining here until the mid-twentieth century.

▼ **Columbus Circle, today.** Skyscrapers such as the Lincoln Center and the Time Warner Center have replaced the tenement buildings. Only Central Park and the USS *Maine* National Monument remain from the early days.

NATIONAL MALL
WASHINGTON, DISTRICT OF COLUMBIA

This concentrated, two-mile east–west expanse of public buildings and manicured grounds was originally a marshy, tidal area flowing into the Potomac River. It was likely used by members of the Nacotchtank tribe as hunting and gathering grounds. By the late 1700s, it was being considered for America's national capital; French engineer Pierre L'Enfant was commissioned to design this new city, and imagined the mall as a long, Parisian-style avenue, with a canal running its length. By 1940, after much political wrangling, as well as

significant dredging to fill in the marsh areas, the mall's revised 1902 design showcased the Lincoln Memorial at one end and the Capitol Building at the other. It has now become a symbolic place of learning, and the site of many gatherings and demonstrations, including Martin Luther King Jr.'s 1963 march for civil rights, where he famously spoke on the steps of the Lincoln Memorial: "I have a dream . . ."

◀ "America's Front Yard," early twentieth century, with the Smithsonian Institution and Capitol Building. The mall was overgrown with trees and gardens at this point, though the revised 1902 design was gaining steam.

▲ The National Mall today, looking east to the Capitol Building from atop the Washington Monument. Buildings seen include the Smithsonian Institution, National Air and Space Museum, National Museum of the American Indian, and National Museum of Art.

PITTSBURGH
PENNSYLVANIA

Famous for Carnegie Hall, Heinz Baked Beans, and artist Andy Warhol, Pittsburgh is also synonymous with the iron and steel industry, which dominated its economy and landscape from the early 1800s right through to the 1970s. Originally inhabited by Algonquian- and Iroquoian-speaking peoples, the Pittsburgh area, by 1761, was known as Fort Pitt. Its European settlers gradually expanded out from the fort, turning the growing town into a key stopping-off point for those heading west after the American Revolution. Not long

after, industrialization and good access to a number of natural resources such as wood and coal turned Pittsburgh into the "Iron City," with steel mills and a thriving, though heavily polluted, urban area. From 1870 to 1910, Pittsburgh's population grew from about 86,000 to over 525,000. However, by the 1980s, much of the industry had left, and the city has turned to lighter industries such as metalworking and plastic manufacture as well as high-tech robotics.

◀ Pittsburgh, 1890; railroads and warehouses crowd the riverfront. Heavily polluted by smokestacks and mills, by 1910, the city produced more than 60 percent of the nation's steel.

▼ Downtown Pittsburgh's Golden Triangle, seen from the Duquesne Incline, a restored wooden cable car opened in 1877 and operating between South Shore and Mount Washington. The fountain marks the point where the Allegheny and Monongahela Rivers join to become the Ohio River.

CHICAGO
ILLINOIS

Chicago, built on the banks of Lake Michigan, is one of America's largest cities, with several iconic downtown areas. These include the Michigan–Wacker Historic District, home to the original site of Fort Dearborn and a smattering of 1920s-built skyscrapers on both sides of the Chicago River. Due to the varying terrain by the river, many streets here are stacked on two or three levels, like a layer cake. The nearby thirteen-block section of North Michigan Avenue, coined the Magnificent Mile, is one of America's most luxurious shopping

avenues, and is home to the Tribune Tower, as well as the Wrigley and Palmolive Buildings. Chicago's commercial center, however, remains the thirty-five-block Loop, named for its original encircling cable-car track. It includes the financial district, Willis Tower, and a pedestrianized walkway along the Chicago River. Among outdoor artworks by the likes of Pablo Picasso, Joan Míro, and Marc Chagall stands Anish Kapoor's gleaming stainless-steel sculpture *Cloudgate*, aka "the Bean."

◀ Looking west on the Chicago River toward the Wabash Avenue Bridge, ca. 1930s. Note the parked cars alongside East Wacker Drive's lower roadway. The north side of the river was still a railyard, with no real pedestrian access to the riverfront.

▲ Looking west from the DuSable Bridge, known locally as the Michigan Avenue Bridge, down the Chicago River; East Wacker Drive hugs the river's south side, now a continuous 1.25-mile pedestrian walkway.

▶ Chicago's Gold Coast, ca. 1935, with Oak Street Beach in the foreground. Lincoln Park is yet to be extended further south. The 1886 lakefront mansion seen in the foreground was demolished in the 1960s to make way for the thiry-six-story Carlyle, Chicago's first luxury high-rise condominium.

▶▶ Looking north toward North Avenue Beach. Piers along the shoreline help hold in the sand from Lake Michigan. The now expanded 1,208-acre Lincoln Park—America's second most visited city park—lies to the left.

CHICAGO'S GOLD COAST Originally a swamp on Chicago's Near North Side, by the 1900s, the Gold Coast had become one of the city's most affluent districts, thanks to millionaire Potter Palmer building his forty-two-room turreted mansion there in the 1880s. One hundred years later, the Gold Coast was one of America's richest neighborhoods and was placed on the National Register of Historic Places. Today, it forms the northern end of the luxury shopping district known as the Magnificent Mile, with the city's Lincoln Park just to the north.

DENVER

COLORADO

Rumors of gold at the foot of the Rocky Mountains brought a stampede of prospectors to what was to become Denver, overrunning the Arapaho tribe who had inhabited the region. An estimated 100,000 people arrived in Colorado between 1858 and 1860. Denver soon became a Wild West town full of saloons, brothels, and shady characters. The town had an unsteady start, with fire, a flash flood, and conflicts with the Cheyenne and Arapaho tribes, but within twenty years of the railroad arriving in 1870, its population had grown

astronomically, from under 5,000 to over 105,000. Today, greater Denver is a vast stretch of suburban communities totaling about 155 square miles. The nearby Rocky Mountains bring a large number of tourists, and the Denver branch of the United States Mint has become America's largest gold depository, producing about half of the coins currently circulating in the United States.

◀ Aerial view of downtown Denver, ca. 1898, likely taken from the capitol building and overlooking what is now Civic Center Park. The domed building, since demolished, is the Arapahoe County Courthouse.

▲ Denver sits 5,280 feet above sea level, earning it the nickname "Mile High City." Seen on the left is the Colorado State Capitol Building with its 24-carat gold-leafed dome. The financial district lies in the distance.

LAS VEGAS
NEVADA

Reportedly the brightest place on earth, the city of Las Vegas in the Mojave Desert is renowned for its lavish entertainment hotels, concerts, and casinos. Originally an oasis for the Anasazi and Paiute tribes, and a resting point for Mormon settlers on the Wagon Trail, Las Vegas was a fairly sleepy place until the construction of the nearby Boulder (now Hoover) Dam started in 1931. Coupled with the legalization of casino gambling, a new crowd of tourists, celebrities, and even the mob arrived, capitalizing on the city's more relaxed views.

In the 1950s, when most of America was still segregated into Black- and white-only areas, the Moulin Rouge became Vegas's first racially integrated casino-hotel. Over the years, thousands of stars have "played" Vegas, including Elvis Presley, Sammy Davis Jr., Prince, and Adele. Las Vegas today is one of America's most visited attractions, receiving many more tourists annually than the Grand Canyon.

◀ Aerial view looking east along Fremont Street, from the Las Vegas Union Pacific train station, ca. 1958. The Mint, Hotel Fremont, Lucky Strike, and Golden Nugget signs can be seen running its length.

▼ Looking south down the Las Vegas Strip, 2009. Visible are Caesar's Palace, the curve of the lit-up Bellagio fountain, and the Eiffel Tower replica at the Paris Las Vegas hotel.

◄ Fremont Street, aka "Glitter Gulch," ca. 1950s, with the Golden Nugget, one of the city's oldest casinos (named for the 18-inch-long gold nugget, known as the Hand of Faith, displayed inside). Vegas Vic waves from his perch on the Pioneer Club, with a "Howdy Pardner!" every fifteen minutes.

▼ The Golden Nugget is now part of the Fremont Street Experience, a pedestrianized entertainment district covering five blocks of Fremont Street since 1994. The 1,375-foot-long video-screen "canopy" is the world's largest, composed of 49.3 million LED lights. The Hand of Faith is still displayed inside.

AMERICAN LANDSCAPES

NIAGARA FALLS
NIAGARA, NEW YORK AND ONTARIO

AMERICAN, BRIDAL VEIL, AND HORSESHOE FALLS

Disgorging more than 750,000 gallons of water per second down a 188-foot drop, Niagara Falls is not just a marvel of geology but a world-famous tourist attraction and major source of hydroelectric power. After the area became a public park in 1885, on each side of the border—the United States with American and Bridal Veil Falls and Canada with Horseshoe Falls—the once-remote spot quickly gained popularity with more adventurous tourists. Its beauty drew

high-profile visitors such as Winston Churchill and Queen Elizabeth II, but also attracted thrill seekers, tightrope walkers, and people "riding" down inside balls and barrels, with varied success. Thankfully, most of today's 12 million annual visitors—many on honeymoon—are content to use its longstanding observation towers or boat rides for a glimpse, though braver ones can take the 150-foot elevator to the foot of the falls and stand behind the wall of water that barrels down at more than 30 feet per second.

◀ Niagara Falls in the nineteenth century. Canada's Horseshoe Falls, extending 2,300 feet across its curve, is more than twice the length of American and Bridal Veil Falls, and is responsible for 90 percent of the water flowing downriver.

▲ Looking across from the U.S. side, with American Falls and Goat Island in the foreground. The water's distinctive green color comes from the volume of dissolved minerals carried along with the water, including finely crushed rock "flour."

◀ Horseshoe Falls, 1954
and now. The natural
"horseshoe" is partly from
erosion over time. Niagara
Falls has receded an
estimated 7 miles since
it was first created in the
Ice Age, 12,500 years ago.
However, engineering
work has slowed this to
1 foot per 10 years.

THE NIAGARA RIVER Four of the five Great Lakes—nearly 20 percent of the world's fresh water—flow into the Niagara River, which in turn flows 38 miles north, from Lake Erie into Lake Ontario. This enormous total drainage area—about 265,000 square miles—not to mention the drop from Niagara Falls, means huge potential energy from hydroelectric power. In fact, thanks to power stations working alongside the river since 1895, the falls can produce more than 4 million kilowatts, and supply about 1 million people with electricity.

Along with the original Ice Age scouring that created the Niagara Gorge, this amount of surging, falling water has also helped create steep cliffs, class 6 rapids, and a natural whirlpool. It does, however, make the river difficult to cross, resulting in a few failed attempts at building bridges over the years, including one that collapsed in a storm, and another destroyed by ice from the river "grabbing" and twisting it out of shape.

◄ Whirlpool Rapids Bridge under construction, ca. 1896. It replaced the world's first working railway suspension bridge, at one time used to help enslaved people reach Canada. The old bridge was replaced piece by piece to allow traffic to continue.

▲ Rainbow Bridge today. Built in 1941 after the Honeymoon Bridge collapsed into the river in 1938, it is within sight of the falls. The international boundary passes through the middle of the bridge, which sports flags on either side to mark it.

▶ Old Faithful Geyser,
ca. 1915. Cars were only
allowed into the park for
the first time in this year,
and drivers had to carry
a spare tire and tools.
Visitors were able to
get much closer to the
main attractions than
they can today.

▶▶ Old Faithful today.
The geyser continues to
shoot boiling water up
to 180 feet into the air
every 60 to 110 minutes,
about twenty times a day
for as long as 5 minutes.
It has spouted more than
1 million times since the
park opened in 1872.

YELLOWSTONE
WYOMING, MONTANA, AND IDAHO

America's first national park, Yellowstone is arguably its most breathtaking, important, and cherished natural place. Used by American Indians for more than 10,000 years, it covers nearly 3,500 square miles—about the size of Puerto Rico—and forms the core of Greater Yellowstone, one of the world's most intact ecosystems. There are around 10,000 hydrothermal features in this World Heritage Site and UNESCO Biosphere Reserve—from technicolor steaming hot springs and spouting geysers to bubbling mud pots and limestone travertine terraces.

Yellowstone holds more than half of the world's geysers alone. This unique landscape is largely the result of a supervolcano beneath the ground, its massive eruptions hundreds of thousands of years ago coating the region with 5,790 square miles of ash, and filling Yellowstone with flowing lava that has shaped its multicolor canyons and lakes today. Magma bubbles as little as 3 miles beneath the surface of Yellowstone in some places. Today, the park is a wildlife haven, with gray wolves reintroduced in 1995, beaver stocks replenished, and bison back from the brink of extinction.

► President Franklin D. Roosevelt at Artist Point, 1937, overlooking the Grand Canyon of the Yellowstone, the 308-foot drop of its Lower Falls in the distance. Volcanic and glacial processes, and the Yellowstone River itself, gouged a 19-mile-long gorge up to 1,200 feet deep and 4,000 feet across in places.

◄ The canyon today, in the north-central part of the park, is largely unchanged. Its multihued brown, green, and dark orange rock is the result of hydrothermally altered sediments and minerals "painting" the canyon over hundreds of thousands of years. Larger rocks are the remnants of erosion-resistant lava.

THOUSAND MILE TREE

HENEFER, UTAH

In 1869, rail workers in eastern Utah's Weber Canyon noticed a tall Douglas fir to the side of the railroad, which happened also to mark the 1,000th mile of tracks they had just laid west from their starting point in Omaha, Nebraska. They hung a sign off its branches, marking it as the "thousand mile tree." The 90-foot-tall tree in this remote valley became witness to America's first transcontinental train route connecting the United States from east to west—which meant a 3,000-mile journey was now cut from taking several months to less

than a week. The tree became feted as a symbol of the westward expansion of America, with trains stopping for passengers to gaze at it. It also proved a target, with some firing shots into its trunk from passing trains. By 1900, the tree had died and was cut down. In 1982, a new tree was planted in its place.

◄ Thousand Mile Tree, not long after the transcontinental railroad opened, in 1869. It is surrounded by a large group of train passengers, including one who has climbed to the top.

▲ The new fir tree, planted in 1982. Passenger trains no longer run on this line, though freight trains continue to use it. This photograph was taken in 2011.

GRAND CANYON
ARIZONA

Formed about 6 million years ago by the Colorado River snaking through and eroding its banks, the 270-mile-long Grand Canyon in northern Arizona is a mile deep in places. One of the biggest canyons in the world, its steep walls expose layers of earth nearly 2 billion years old, giving archaeologists great insight into the planet's evolutionary history. Its popularity grew with the arrival of the train near the rim in 1902. Train passengers would then use guides with pack mules or horses to descend a trail to the canyon's bottom.

They would stay overnight at Phantom Ranch, still the only accommodation below the canyon rim. The canyon has been inhabited since the last ice age, when prehistoric humans would have hunted mammoths and other long-extinct mammals. For more than 800 years, the Havasupai have lived in and around the canyon, regaining some of their land from the park in 1975.

◀ Early tourists at Bright Angel Point on the canyon's North Rim, in 1922, three years after the Grand Canyon became a national park. Although hard to reach, this was where most travelers started their descent to the canyon bottom.

▼ One of the most popular viewpoints, Bright Angel Point overlooks Bright Angel Canyon and Transept Canyon. The eroded layers of sediment on its ridges are clearly visible.

▶ The 6.6-million-ton Hoover Dam, previously Boulder Dam, 1935, looking toward what will become Lake Mead, America's largest reservoir by volume.

▶▶ Hoover Dam today. Lake Mead's mineralized white "bathtub ring" is normally underwater. However, a "megadrought" has drastically reduced the reservoir's water levels, threatening the operation of the hydroelectric turbines that require the water to be 1,000 feet above sea level.

HOOVER DAM
BLACK CANYON, NEVADA AND ARIZONA

Hearing of possible work on Boulder Dam, thousands of people, many desperate, converged on Las Vegas in 1930, squatting in camps until nearby Boulder City was built for the lucky 21,000 who landed a job. It was dangerous work. More than 100 workers died—including "high scalers," who dangled from ropes at a great height, clearing the canyon walls of debris. Their toil, however, made Hoover Dam (its official name since 1937) an engineering masterpiece—726 feet high and 1,244 feet long at the crest—with a hydroelectric power plant generating electricity for 1 million. Its reservoir, Lake Mead, can hold more than 9 trillion gallons of water, irrigate 1.5 million acres of land, and provide water for 1.6 million, greatly contributing to the development of Las Vegas, Phoenix, and Los Angeles. By its completion in 1936, the concrete arch-gravity dam was the world's highest, using 5 million barrels of concrete and 45 million tons of reinforced steel.

▲ The nearly completed Hoover Dam in 1935. Its opening in 1936 was commemorated by U.S. president Franklin D. Roosevelt, and watched by a crowd of 20,000. It was built at enormous cost, but paid for itself, with interest, by 1987, thanks to sales of the electrical power it had generated.

▶ Aerial view of the dam today. Vehicle traffic between Nevada and Arizona drove along the dam's crest until a 1,060-foot concrete-arch bridge—the longest of its type in North America—was built in 2010 (seen in the background here).

▶▶ Hoover Dam construction. Top left: Black Canyon, looking upstream on the Colorado River, 1930. Top right: Temporary footbridge and steel suspension bridge and the 56-inch diversion tunnels used to carry the river water while the dam was being constructed, ca. 1932. Bottom left: Four tons of dynamite helped clear the rock, 1933. Bottom right: The dam today, with the power station set within huge concrete blocks.

YOSEMITE

CALIFORNIA

Sitting in the heart of California's Sierra Nevada mountains, Yosemite played host to a significant camping trip by President Theodore Roosevelt in 1903, where he was inspired by Yosemite's wilderness to enlarge the park as well as sign five new national parks, eighteen national monuments, fifty-five national bird sanctuaries and wildlife refuges, and 150 national forests into existence. Bounded on all sides by forest, this 1,200-square-mile landscape—nearly 8 miles east to west—has been shaped over millions of years by glaciers and erosion,

revealing unique granite formations and waterfalls. It claims
five of the world's highest waterfalls, including the 2,400-foot-
high Yosemite Falls, and its immense granite monoliths such
as the 3,600-foot-high El Capitan are a rock-climbing hub.
Closer to the ground, the UNESCO World Heritage Site's
more than 500 mature giant sequoia trees—some up to
209 feet tall and 100-feet wide at the base—are a major draw
for the park's 3 million annual visitors.

◀ The first automobiles driving in a convoy into Yosemite Valley,
June 2, 1915, over the Wawona Road. The valley itself is about
7 miles long and 1 mile across in some places.

▲ The view today is unchanged, with the sheer granite walls
of El Capitan on the left, Clouds Rest peak and Half Dome
in the distance, and the Cathedral Rocks trio of peaks and
620-foot-high Bridalveil Fall to the right.

► Defying warning signs such as "It is 3,000 feet to the bottom and no undertaker to meet you," visitors pose for a photo on Glacier Point's Overhanging Rock, about 3,200 feet above Yosemite Valley, ca. 1887. Spurred on, other tourists would perform acrobatics and even drive their car right up to the edge.

◄ Though experienced climbers may still dare to reach Overhanging Rock, the safer viewing platform of Glacier Point is a more popular choice. It commands an equally inspiring bird's-eye view of Yosemite Valley with the Sierra Nevada mountains in the distance, complete with the spectacular Half Dome granite outcrop.

OCEAN BEACH
SAN FRANCISCO, CALIFORNIA

Originally a 3.5-mile expanse of rolling sand dunes and coastal scrub used by the Yelamu Tribe of the Ohlone Nation and then Spanish settlers, the Ocean Beach area was dubbed the "outside lands" in the early 1800s for its inhospitable climate—it was foggy, windy, and had dangerous, cold waters. By the late 1800s, it was known as "Carville," a 2,000-strong community of unique homes and businesses made from retired horse-drawn streetcars. With the city's changeover to electric streetcars, the old ones were going cheap. Thanks partly to the

draw of the adjacent Golden Gate Park, by the 1920s, though Carville had been mostly dismantled, Ocean Beach was a thriving tourist spot, with a large public swimming pool, restaurants, nightclubs, and a 10-acre amusement park called Playland. By the 1940s, it became a surfing destination, and is where the wet suit was invented. Today, the beach and park are considered one of San Francisco's best outdoor spaces.

◄ Ocean Beach, ca. 1935. Playland sits to the left, with the Great Highway adjacent, built in 1929. In the distance, on either side of Golden Gate Park, sit a pair of windmills, built in 1903 to pump water throughout its grounds.

▲ Ocean Beach today, with its characteristic fog in the distance. Golden Gate Park and the windmills remain, though Playland has been replaced by residential housing. The north windmill was restored in 1981.

HI-FI HOUSE

hi-fi music

AMERICA ON THE MOVE

SOUTH STATION
BOSTON, MASSACHUSETTS

When it opened in 1899, South Station was the world's largest train station. Set on 35 acres adjacent to Fort Point Channel, nearby streets were rerouted for its construction and a seawall built to hold back the water. The five-story Neoclassical Revival–style building held twenty-eight tracks at ground level and four beneath, enclosed by a massive roof. The main waiting room was 225 by 65 feet (the women's was 34 by 44 feet), with marble mosaic floors. The lunchroom stools and counters were made from Tennessee marble and mahogany, and the station's

forty-five bathrooms had automatically flushing toilets. By 1913, it was the world's busiest station, seeing 38 million passengers a year. In 1945, GIs returning after World War II took this figure to 135,000 passengers a day. Yet, by the 1960s, passengers numbered only 4.5 million a year—scheduled for demolition, the station's headhouse and waiting room were saved and placed on the National Register of Historic Places.

◀ **South Station, ca. 1900.** Its exterior clock was the second-largest of its kind in the United States at the time, with a 12-foot-wide face and a minute hand 6 feet long. The eagle statue above it has an 8-foot wingspan.

▼ **South Station today, the original facade unchanged.** Its grounds now form part of a larger subway system, the entrance seen here out front. The clock is the original, and is hand-wound twice a week.

JFK AIRPORT
NEW YORK CITY, NEW YORK

When 4,930-acre Idlewild Airport, officially known as New York International Airport, opened on the south shore of Queens in 1948, about 215,000 people came to watch the opening ceremony, which included the largest flyover of military aircraft in peacetime. It quickly became known as one of the world's most state-of-the-art international airports, continuing to build and extend its runways throughout the 1950s and 1960s, and changing its name to John F. Kennedy Airport in 1963 to honor the assassinated president. Its

innovative Terminal City allowed each airline to design its own terminal, leading to iconic structures and inventions such as boarding bridges, conveyor-belt luggage claim, and supermarket-style checkouts. Employing around 35,000 people, it remains one of the world's busiest airports—in 2018, it had 61.6 million passengers, double that of 2003, with 455,524 flights and nearly 1.5 tons of cargo.

◄ TWA Flight Center exterior, 1963, one year after opening. This neo-futuristic structure was designed by renowned Finnish-American architect Eero Saarinen, who wanted its shape to reflect a bird with its wings spread in flight.

▲ TWA Hotel exterior, 2019. The old terminal has been reimagined as a 512-room hotel. Its additional buildings and renovation—costing some $265 million—places it as one of the world's most expensive airport hotels.

▼ TWA Flight Center interior, 1960s, featuring distinctive
curved glass walls, staircases, and ceilings. Known as the
"Grand Central of the Jet Age" when it opened in 1962, the
terminal remained in service until 2001.

▼   TWA Hotel lobby interior, 2019. The Sunken Lounge, where
crowds gathered to watch the Beatles first arrive in 1965, has
been authentically restored. The electronic board that once
displayed flight schedules is now part of the check-in desk.

ELLIS ISLAND
NEW YORK CITY, NEW YORK

It is thought that about 40 percent of U.S. citizens can trace an ancestor to Ellis Island. Its original 3.3 acres, sitting in New York Harbor 1 mile from Manhattan, were first used by Algonquian-speaking tribes for their oyster beds but had become the site of a U.S. military fort by the 1800s. Infill doubled the island's size by 1892, and it became a U.S. immigration station, processing some 400,000 people in its first year. Verifying paperwork and checking for contagious diseases usually took three to seven hours, though some people

were detained for days or even weeks. In 1907, 1.2 million came through its doors, hoping to immigrate to America, though by the 1920s, restrictive quotas meant there were more deportations than admissions. By the time it closed in 1954, Ellis Island had gained 24 acres in landfill, though its 250 employees almost outnumbered detained immigrants. Now a museum, it was substantially restored in 1990 at a cost of $156 million.

◀ Aerial view of Ellis Island, 1936. Restrictive quotas in the 1920s saw fewer admissions, particularly among those from eastern and southern Europe. Thousands who were not admitted were then stranded on the island, awaiting deportation.

▲ Aerial view of Ellis Island today, with Manhattan in the distance. A lawsuit in 1998 determined that New York could retain the island's original 3.3 acres, with the additional landfilled acres belonging to New Jersey.

The noisy Great Hall, or Registry Room, early 1900s, where immigrants crowd its long benches, awaiting inspection. From 1900 to 1924, up to 5,000 people a day were examined in this room, 202 feet long by 102 feet wide. Today, the restored hall is part of the island's larger museum.

GRAND CENTRAL TERMINAL
NEW YORK CITY, NEW YORK

Backdrop and inspiration for movies, books, poems, and TV shows, Manhattan's Grand Central Terminal remains the world's largest, and one of its busiest, train stations. When it opened in 1913, it was among the first all-electric buildings, with chandeliers and lighting fixtures featuring bare bulbs, and its use of ramps to help passengers with luggage was soon copied by stations around the world. Made a National Historic Landmark in 1976, it has since been renovated, its vast Main Concourse restored to its 1913 splendor.

◀ **Woman sitting on luggage in Grand Central Terminal, 1958.** Each face on the four-sided clock at the information booth was made of opal, making it one of the world's most expensive.

▲ **Main Concourse today.** The clock, now worth up to $20 million, remains, and the grime obscuring the celestial ceiling has been removed. It shows not the stars as you might see them from Earth, but as if looking down on Earth.

◄ Grand Central Terminal, on Pershing Square, with Park Avenue Viaduct to the right, 1940s and today. The terminal facade, with its 48-foot-wide sculpture *Glory of Commerce*, 13-foot-wide clock, and three arched windows, remains unchanged, though Pershing Square, once a bus station, is now a pedestrian plaza.

PENN STATION
NEW YORK CITY, NEW YORK

The Beaux Arts Penn Station, partly modeled on the UK's Bank of England building, covered acres of midtown Manhattan, with 148-foot-high ceilings and a canopy of iron and glass for its train platforms. It rivaled Grand Central—receiving 109 million passengers a year in 1945—yet was demolished in the 1960s to be replaced by an unattractive and much-maligned modern building. Its original destruction ushered in a new recognition of the need to protect New York's older buildings, and the city's Landmarks Preservation

Commission was created a year later. The organization was instrumental in preserving Grand Central Terminal from the same fate. During its demolition, Penn Station rented out its airspace to sports complex Madison Square Garden, which was built over the top and remains today. Thanks to the redevelopment of a historic building next door, Penn Station has a new main concourse, with a glass atrium and echoes of the previous building's high ceilings.

◀ **Main concourse of Penn Station, 1911. At this point, it was receiving 10 million passengers a year and had been designed to withstand 200,000 travelers a day for the next 100 years.**

▼ **Moynihan Train Hall, 2020, built inside the old United States Postal Service building across the street. On the National Register of Historic Places and opened in 1914, the renovated 32,000-square-foot building now forms part of Penn Station.**

▲ Aerial view of Penn Station in the 1950s, stretching two city
blocks between Seventh and Eighth Avenues between 31st and
33rd Streets. Its classical facade dominates, its glass and steel
train canopy aglow against the New York skyline. The Empire
State Building can be seen in the distance.

◀ Madison Square Garden, entertainment venue and home of the Knicks and the Rangers, seen from the thirty-sixth floor of the New Yorker Hotel today. It sits above Penn Station, with the new Moynihan Train Hall to its right (out of view). The 750-foot-tall One Penn Plaza stands in the foreground on the left.

UNION STATION
DENVER, COLORADO

Without navigable rivers, Denver relied heavily on the railroad for its initial expansion, but the town had several stations, with tricky connections due to rickety unpaved roads. To consolidate these trains in one place, the Denver Union Depot was built in 1881, and signified the town's growing importance as a link between east and west. No expense was spared, with a 180-foot-tall clock tower and an exterior of pink-gray rhyolite and pink sandstone trim. It was the tallest building in the west in its day. After an electrical fire started by a chandelier led to it

being partially consumed by fire in 1894, the central portion was rebuilt in 1914. The granite exterior was designed in a Beaux Arts style with a glass and metal marquee on the first floor. By the mid-1940s, the station had more than 50,000 visitors daily. After falling into decline toward the end of the twentieth century, the building was redeveloped in 2014 as a hub for shopping, dining, and culture.

◀ Union Station, with a metal welcome arch on the right, 1910s. The words "Welcome" and "Mizpah" were written on it, *mizpah* meaning "watchtower" in Hebrew, explaining the emotional bond that continues when people are separated. The arch was torn down in 1933.

▲ Union Station after redevelopment, 2016. The building now houses a hotel and retail space, with a redesigned public square out front. The neon "Union Station—Travel by Train" sign, added in 1953, remains.

DRIVE-THRU TREES
CALIFORNIA

The three remaining "drive-thru" trees are found in Northern California. They are all coastal redwoods, the slimmer and taller of two sequoia species that grow so large it seemed a logical step for humans to tunnel, then drive, through them as a tourist attraction. These trees can live up to 2,200 years and grow to enormous heights—a 380-foot coastal redwood is the world's tallest tree. The other two drive-thru trees— since fallen—were giant sequoias, which can live up to 3,000 years and are only found in about seventy-three groves on the Sierra Nevada's slopes, many in Yosemite National Park. Still alive, however, and without a hole through it, is giant sequoia General Sherman, one of Earth's largest living organisms, with a base girth of more than 100 feet. These trees can resprout at their base if burned in wildfires, with protective bark to withstand flames, pests, and diseases. Almost all old-growth sequoias have been logged; the remaining few are preserved in parks.

◄ Driving through the 234-foot-tall, 2,100-year-old Wawona Tree in Yosemite National Park, ca. 1920, and the tree today, which fell in a storm in 1969. The tunnel was 7 feet wide, 9 feet high, and 26 feet long at the base.

◀ A family parked under the 315-foot-tall Chandelier Tree, Leggett, California, ca. 1950, and the same tree today, which receives about 500 cars daily. The tree, with a circumference of 70 feet, was first carved in 1937.

SANTA FE DEPOT
SAN DIEGO, CALIFORNIA

Santa Fe Depot, California's third busiest train station, is a beautifully built reminder of the area's Spanish and Mexican heritage, as well as its earlier attempts to become the Pacific rail destination of choice. Its predecesor, an 1887 Victorian-style wooden station, had failed to become the western terminus of the Continental Railway, though it certainly brought new residents: between 1880 and 1890, San Diego, once a fishing village, grew sixfold. Today's six-track replacement station was built in 1915 alongside an exposition

celebrating the opening of the Panama Canal. Designed in
a Spanish Colonial Revival style, it features two distinctive
campanile towers with colorful tiled domes, a Spanish tiled
roof, whitewashed walls, and a 650-foot-long wooden
concourse. Its main waiting room still has its redwood-beam
ceiling and hundred-year-old oak benches. Saved from
demolition in the 1970s, it has nearly 450,000 passengers
a year, many of whom take the scenic route along the coast
to Los Angeles.

◀ A crowd at Santa Fe Depot, ca. 1915–20. Its row of large palms
was saved when the old station was demolished, to be replanted
next to the new station concourse.

▲ Santa Fe Depot, 2013, its 1950s blue-and-white "Santa Fe" sign
at center. Restored to its 1914 appearance, the station now
houses a branch of the Museum of Contemporary Art and
features a local trolley line.

CABLE CARS
SAN FRANCISCO, CALIFORNIA

San Franciscan cable cars are known throughout the world for their distinctive design and are synonymous with the hilly California city. The cable-driven rail system, which pulls cars along by cables running beneath the street, was first run in 1873. These vehicles are true survivors: they got through the 1906 earthquake and fires that devastated most of San Francisco, and—thanks to huge community and nationwide support from celebrities and even *Life* magazine—they saw off attempts in the 1940s to replace them with electric streetcars.

In the 1940s, the first African American streetcar conductor was none other than the famous writer Maya Angelou. The car requires two people to operate: a conductor and a gripman, who uses a device to "grip" the cable as it runs under the track at 9.5 miles per hour—this is no small feat with a car that weighs 8 tons when empty. Today, San Francisco has three cable lines, wildly popular with visitors and beloved by locals.

◀ An operator turns a Powell–Mason line cable car on a revolving platform among San Francisco traffic, ca. 1955. For years, the city gave the "best cable car and trolley operator of the year" an all-expenses-paid trip to Hawaii.

▼ Antique cable car, Powell–Mason line, Market Street, 2014. This smaller type of cable car needs turntables set in the street to reverse direction at the ends of the line.

▲ San Francisco cable car, ca. 1925. Derided by newspapers as an "experiment in socialism," cable cars were part of the first metropolitan street railway to be owned and operated by the people of an American city.

◀ San Francisco cable car today. The famous brass bell on top of the cable car has a story of its own—conductors have competed in an informal bell-ringing contest for more than fifty years.

GAS STATIONS AND DINERS
NATIONWIDE

Few icons represent America better than its historic gas stations and diners. Dining cars originated in about 1890, as horse-drawn wagons repurposed to serve "fast" food late into the night. The first stationary diner arrived in 1913, and by the 1930s, many sported the chrome interiors and bullet-shaped design so familiar today. Gas stations emerged as filling stations outside city centers between 1907 and 1913. They soon became mini retail hubs and, often, beacons along seemingly endless, lonely stretches of road.

◀ **Conoco Tower Station and U-Drop Inn, Shamrock, Texas, 1930s, built in 1936 at the junction between historic Route 66 and US 83. Designer John Nunn drew its original plans in the dirt with an old nail.**

▼ **Art Deco U-Drop Inn, today. It appears as Ramone's House of Body Art in the 2006 film *Cars*. The neon has been restored and the diner is now a visitor center for the city of Shamrock.**

▼ Lindholm Oil Company Service Station, Cloquet, Minnesota, post-1968. Designed by Frank Lloyd Wright in 1927, it was not built until 1958, when Wright designed owner R. W. Lindholm's house and convinced him to use this design for his gas station.

▼ Lindholm Oil Company Service Station, 2020, now run by original owner R. W. Lindholm's grandson. Wright's distinctive design includes a glass observation deck, still present, where attendants can watch for cars in comfort.

▲ Mickey's Diner, downtown St. Paul, Minnesota, 1983. The thirty-six-seat all-night eatery, with eighteen counter stools and four booths, was opened in 1939 when owner Bert Mattson parked his 50-foot dining car at Ninth Street and stayed put. It is listed in the National Register of Historic Places.

▲ Mickey's Diner, today. The street has been renamed, with countless buildings demolished and replaced with skyscrapers. The iconic dining car closed its doors in 2020, after eighty years of serving home-cooked food to shift workers and night owls, though plans are afoot for a reopening.

INDEX

PICTURE CREDITS

The publisher would like to thank the following for the permission to reproduce copyrighted material.

123RF:
Jiawangkun: 81.

Alamy:
American Photo Archive: 21 (left); Chronicle: 80; Lucy Clark: 2 (right), 70 (right), 71 (bottom); ClassicStock: 7 (left), 8–9, 22, 134 (left), 135 (top); Orjan Ellingvag: 125; Everett Collection Historical: 12; imageBROKER: 45; Imago History Collection: 30; Evgeny Ivanov: 142 (bottom); Kirby Lee: 69; Norman Pogson: 77; Ian Shipley ARC: 139; Sipa US: 32 (right), 33 (bottom); Sueddeutsche Zeitung Photo: 110; SuperStock: 90, 92; David Wall: 53; Charles Wollertz: 127.

Bibliothèque nationale de France: 64.

Dreamstime:
Felix Mizioznikov: 57.

Getty Images:
Archive Photos: 143 (top), 148; Authenticated News: 44; Bettmann: 2 (left), 20, 21 (top right), 38, 40, 46, 56, 66, 70 (left), 71 (top), 76, 84, 98 (left), 99 (top), 104, 113 (bottom left), 118, 128, 142 (top), 146, 154; brandstaetter images: 86; Buyenlarge: 42; ClassicStock: 18; Fotosearch: 82; R. Gates: 138; General Photographic Agency: 113 (top left); Chris Graythen: 65; Emil Otto Hoppe/Ullstein bild: 54–55, 72, 156–157; Hulton Archive: 50, 112 (left); Jayne Kamin-Oncea: 73; Gary Kellner: 63; Gene Lester: 68; Library of Congress: 74–75, 88, 144; New York Daily News Archive: 60; The New York Historical Society: 136; Joe Daniel Price: 28 (right), 29 (bottom); Print Collector: 96; George Rinhart: 140; Underwood Archives: 34, 78; Universal History Archive: 48.

J. Paul Getty Museum:
Digital image courtesy of the Getty's Open Content Program: 106.

iStock:
burwellphotography: 31; Eloi_Omella: 13; Fischerrx6: 19; Littleny: 137; OlegAlbinsky: 21 (bottom right); Pgiam: 7 (right), 24 (left), 25 (bottom), 134 (right), 135 (bottom); Starcevic: 85.

Library of Congress, Washington D.C.:
10, 14 (left), 15 (top), 16, 24 (right), 25 (top), 26, 28 (left), 29 (top), 32 (left), 33 (top), 36, 58, 62, 91, 94–95, 108, 113 (top right), 116, 120–121, 122, 124, 126, 132, 152, 158–159.

The New York Public Library:
The Miriam and Ira D. Wallach Division of Art, Prints and Photographs: Photography Collection: 130 (left), 131 (top).

NPS Photo:
Yellowstone National Park Archive: 102; Yosemite National Park Archive: 114.

Shutterstock:
Alisa_Ch: 143 (bottom); Rudy Balasko: 37, 39; Marcio Jose Bastos Silva: 123; Iris van den Broek: 155; Canadastock: 117; Richard Cavalleri: 61; Checubus: 83; Engel Ching: 49; Rob Crandall: 130 (right), 131 (bottom); Cvandyke: 35; Everett Historical: 52; f11photo: 103; Ken Felepchuk: 101; Sergii Figurnyi: 113 (bottom right); frank_peters: 23; gabriel12: 59; Diego Grandi: 51; Arina P. Habich: 141; Hakat: 93; Iv-olga: 105; JamesChen: 109; Nick Martinson: 41; Linda McKusick: 153; Melpomene: 79; Felix Mizioznikov: 129; Diego de Munari: 98 (right), 99 (bottom); Trong Nguyen: 43; Jam Norasett: 97; Timothy OLeary: 112 (right); Oscity: 14 (right), 15 (bottom); Sean Pavone: 11, 27, 47; Frank Romeo: 67; Roschetzky Photography: 89; SergiyN: 87; Alexander Sloutsky: 119; Stolnikphotography: 149; T Photography: 151; Gary C. Tognoni: 115; Travelview: 145; Tupungato: 111; Marc Venema: 17; Wangkun Jia: 147.

Texas Historical Commission: 150.

Unsplash: Stephen H: 133.

While every effort has been made to credit photographers, The Bright Press would like to apologize should there have been any omissions or errors, and would be pleased to make the appropriate correction for future editions of the book.